The Woman I Fell in Love With

A Woman's Guide to Self-Love

www.KedraSpeaks1.com

AUTOGRAPH

Brittney,

Go After Your Dreams!!

Kecia Speaks

THE WOMAN I FELL IN LOVE WITH
A Woman's Guide to Self-Love
Kedra Speaks

Copyright © 2016 by Kedra Speaks Organization

Printed in the United States of America

ISBN-13: 978-0692756508
ISBN-10: 0692756507

Cover Photo by Raphael Gentry @ RMG Media

Editing, Formatting, and Cover Concept/Design by:

SD Horton Enterprises

P.O. Box 1612

Alamogordo, NM 88311

www.sdhortonenterprises.com

All rights reserved. No portion of this book may be used without permission of the author or publisher, with the exception of brief excerpts for magazine articles, reviews, etc.

TABLE OF CONTENTS

A Letter to My Mother   iv
From Jada Reeves

A Letter to My Daughter   vi

Acknowledgements   vii

Introduction   ix

Chapter 1: Love Yourself   1

Chapter 2: Know Who You Are   7

Chapter 3: It's Not Where You Start, But Where You Finish   11

Chapter 4: Know What Time It Is   17

Chapter 5: Trust The Vision   25

Chapter 6: Keep Your Cup Full   31

Chapter 7: Be A Woman Of Influence   35

Chapter 8: Know When To Let Go   41

Chapter 9: Believe In Yourself   45

Chapter 10: Don't Give Up   49

Chapter 11: Show Up   55

Chapter 12: Set Standards   61

Chapter 13: Have Faith   65

Chapter 14: Never Settle   69

My Family

Biography

A LETTER TO MY MOTHER

By Jada Reeves

I am writing a letter to my mother because she deserves to know how I feel about her. She's so nice and down to earth, but don't get on her bad side. She makes me feel like the funniest person on earth as if I am Kevin Hart's daughter. She laughs at my jokes even if they are corny. A lady who pushes me to do my best at all times. She explains why being successful is so important. She just wants the best for everyone. She's the one who everyone calls for advice and when they need someone to talk to. After you get finished talking to her, you will feel so much better, as if God has talked to you Himself. She makes sure she has done the right thing at all times because if I'm not watching her, someone else is. She reminds me in the real world it is not going to be easy and the world does not revolve around me. So I have to toughen up now. She shows me that all I have to do is keep walking by faith and I'll be good. When we moved to Atlanta, all we had was our clothes. I don't know how we did it but we did; and if that's not walking by faith then I don't know what is. What I am trying to explain is she is the hardest working, most dedicated, loving, caring, and helpful person I know. That's why I love her!! Thanks mother for everything you do.

A Letter to My Daughter

Daughter, one of the things I want you to know is that no matter what you go through in life, your future will be bright. You are beautiful, smart, and unstoppable! There is nothing in this world that you can't do. Whatever you set your mind on, be sure to work hard to achieve your goals and you will go far in life. As a young lady, there will be times when you will be challenged to do things that you may feel uncomfortable doing or not doing. Learn to spend time with yourself and learn how to love yourself. Loving yourself is not just getting your hair or your nails done. It is being selective of the choices you make. When you love yourself, there are certain things that you just won't do; there are certain things that you will not allow to happen. Fall in love with every aspect of you and **GO DO YOU!** You have everything you need on the inside of you to make your life phenomenal!! I hope these words have inspired you to love yourself before you even attempt to love anyone else.

ACKNOWLDEGEMENTS

First and foremost, I would like to thank God for His grace and mercy. I would like to thank Him for always keeping me in and out of the storm. I would like to thank all the people who have supported me on my journey. First of all, I would like to thank my mother Demelody Terry for believing in me, and for giving birth to me...an awesome gift from God. Kedra is the name my mama gave me & speaking is my gift from God, so I will always be Kedra Speaks! I would like to thank my children, Dre, Javares, and Jada for always believing in me. I have a section in here with my children. My daughter said to me that I did not discuss her enough in the book so towards the end of me finishing up this book, I wrote about her. They are my reasons for being; they are my source of inspiration. I would like to thank my mother for giving me life and wings to fly. I would like to thank my four sisters for always being in my corner. I would like to thank my special friend Rondalynn Warrior for believing in my dream and being there throughout this process to answer my texts and phone calls. I would like to thank all the angels God has camped up around me. Every time I started to doubt, an angel would appear through phone calls, texts and even in person to remind me of my why. I would like to thank all the people who told me **NO** so that I could get my Yes!!

Introduction

When I first set out to write a book, I had no idea on what to write about. Let me re-phrase that. I had many ideas, but none of them were making sense into how I would tie them altogether. But one day after attending an entrepreneur initiative, and receiving advice from a business coach and speaker, it hit me. I came home, sat down, and began to write and the words started to flow freely. This is for anyone who may consider writing a book and may be stuck on what to write about. Write about what you know, write about your truth, tell your story and know that no one can tell your story like you. I hope that this book will inspire women of all ages around the world. Considering the life that I have lived and struggled with self-love, I hope that these words will help women to get in touch with their inner self and find love just where you are. You may not be the reddest apple on the tree but that does not mean that you don't have value. No matter where you are in life, always remember that you do have value. Value yourself and hold a high standard for your life. This will take you far. Even in a dry spell, you still have something to give. You may not have all the money in the world, but you do have something to offer to the world. This is my gift that I am offering to you!

CHAPTER

-1-

LOVE YOURSELF

1

LOVE YOURSELF

So many women run from the woman who they were meant to be. I was one of those women. I knew everything I did not want to be, but I did not know who I wanted to be. Everybody has an idea of who they want to be when they grow up. Some want to grow up to be doctors, lawyers, or some other type of professional. At the age of 15, I happened to have gotten pregnant and stopped dreaming, so I never knew who I wanted to be when I grew up. Like many of you reading this book, maybe a life situation happened and you have stopped dreaming. Maybe you had

THE WOMAN I FELL IN LOVE WITH

a baby, maybe you lost a job, or maybe you lost a love one, and you don't know where to pick up the pieces. It's never too late to start dreaming again. After having my son, I knew everything that I did not want to be. I did not want to be a statistic, and I did not want to be a single mom raising children on her own because I watched how my mom struggled.

I did not want to be viewed as a failure. But as time went on, and after making several mistakes along the way, I ended up being everything that I did not want to be. After 2 failed marriages, here I am—a single mother living in a 3 bedroom apartment just like my mom. But what I found out in this process is this is exactly who I needed to be in order to fall deeply in love with myself and be the woman that God has called me to be.

You see, sometimes God will allow you to take the long route just so you can get where He wants you to be. That's exactly what He did with me. So all the highs and lows were necessary in order for me to become the woman that I

Love Yourself

am today! The woman I am today is the woman I fell deeply in love with and she is all the woman that I need. She is confident, she is sexy, and she is smart! Never let a situation or a setback dictate your life. Everything you are going through is preparing you for where you are meant to be.

THE WOMAN I FELL IN LOVE WITH

WAYS TO SELF LOVE

Repeat these daily mantras:

1. I will not talk negative to myself.

2. I will walk away from anything that does not serve me.

3. I will put myself at the top of my to-do list.

I will practice self- love by:

1. _____

   _____

   _____

2. _____

   _____

   _____

3. _____

   _____

   _____

CHAPTER

-2-

KNOW WHO YOU ARE

2

KNOW WHO YOU ARE

We live in a world where people will always try to tell you who you are. According to some people, *You are too skinny, you are too smart, or you will never be good enough.* But God made you just the way you are for a reason, and to fulfill your purpose. Knowing who you are is so important as you walk in this journey of life. Not knowing who you are can be detrimental. It can cost you your joy, your peace, and even much of your money. You may ask, *"How can it cost me money?"* If you are not sure of who you

THE WOMAN I FELL IN LOVE WITH

are, you will spend money on things that you don't need, trying to impress people who you don't even like and people who don't even like you. A high percentage of us (women) spend money on things, such as designer handbags, to validate who we are and to make us look good on the outside while we are struggling with who we are on the inside. Who you are on the inside is more important than what the outer appearance looks like.

I always tell my children to know who they are so that no matter what someone else says, they can be sure of themselves. It is very important that you get your heart right on the inside and learn how to love yourself just as you are. Once you attain a healthy self-esteem about yourself, all the things on the inside will start to show on the outside. So how do you develop a healthy self-esteem? You first start by prayer and supplication. Only God can mend a broken heart. Only God can take you from being bitter, to better. You have to seek God for all the things you need. Forgiveness is the gift you give yourself. If you are walking around angry and with unforgiveness in your heart, those things will be revealed in how you treat others. If you ask God to give you a clean heart (one that is pure), you can then experience all the things that God has for you.

CHAPTER

-3-

IT'S NOT WHERE YOU START, BUT WHERE YOU FINISH

3

IT'S NOT WHERE YOU START, BUT WHERE YOU FINISH

I know many of you reading this book may have come from broken backgrounds and have a long family history of generational curses. Unknowingly, you may be a part of a family comprised of people who are or were overcome with depression, poverty, and lack. Subsequently, you may believe that is the way life is suppose to be and that you can't break free from the barriers that have held you down. I am here to tell you that God's word says that you can have a life of abundance if you believe. It's not where you start,

THE WOMAN I FELL IN LOVE WITH

but where you finish. Maybe you are like me—where your life started in a small town in a place where there are not many opportunities for advancement or financial growth. But, just because your life started that way doesn't mean it has to end as such. Even the bible encourages us to not despise the day of small beginnings.

Maybe your ancestors struggled to overcome obstacles and, as a result of the generation curses, you can't see a light at the end of the tunnel. I am here to tell you that there is a light, and that light is the LORD God Almighty! Develop a close and personal relationship with God and start to seek Him for all of your heart's desires. God is the only one who can take you from where you been to where you want and need to be.

Baby steps count, so start now by making necessary steps toward the goals that you want to achieve. Be intentional about what you want, then go after it with all of your might! You may not currently possess the knowledge needed to obtain the things you desire. If you don't possess this knowledge, you can take a class, sign up for school, and/or even seek a qualified mentor. A mentor is someone who can help you reach your dreams. Find someone who has already attained the experience in walking the path that you desire to walk. Google search can be an essential tool for you to use to research and find out as much information as you can about the dream you want to accomplish. Remember, if you don't know what you need to know, you just don't know! But that is still not a valid excuse for not finding out!

Let me share with you about where I came from that brought me to the point of writing this book. My grandmother Rebecca "Honey" Terry was a single mother of 11 children, but her being single was not by choice. My grandfather passed away and went on to be with the Lord, which made her a widow woman. In spite of this challenge, she did not give up; she still had 11 children to raise by herself. She did not seek out help from another man. In fact, I do not even think she took the time to date again. I

THE WOMAN I FELL IN LOVE WITH

believe her sole purpose, which became her primary focus, was to raise her children. Some of you reading this book may be alone raising your children. I shared this story to let you know that if my grandmother can raise 11 children, you can clearly do your part without any excuses.

You may have had a rough past, and maybe your parents didn't have much money. Maybe you come from a long line of family members who struggled with drug use and alcoholism; but again, its not where you start— it's where you finish. You can get back up and pursue your dreams. Don't ever let your past determine your future. I hope this chapter has inspired you go after your dreams and finish strong!

START WITH WHO YOU ARE

I AM:

_____

_____

_____

MY DREAMS ARE TO BE:

_____

_____

_____

_____

CHAPTER

-4-

KNOW WHAT TIME IT IS

4

KNOW WHAT TIME IT IS

This chapter is special to me because I get to talk about my dad, Michael Copeland (Fluffy), and share this special story. When I was a little girl, I was very sensitive and would cry just about anything. I remember my dad would come to pick me up, and we would go for a ride in his car. We would talk about life and different things; and some of those things made me cry. He would always say to me *"You got to know what time it is."* I always wondered what he was talking about. My dad was not a spiritual man, but as I have become an adult, I have come to realize that he must know the word of God to some extent because what he said translates to what's written in the following scripture. Ecclesiastes 3:1 says: *"There is a time for everything, and a season for every activity under the heavens: a time to be born and a time to die; a time to plant and a time to uproot."* You get the picture? So, there will be times in our lives where we will have to determine if or when it is time to leave, or stay in a relationship. We will have to determine if or when it is time to stay, or walk away from a job. Either way, we will have to know what time it is.

As I am writing this book, I am being faced with the challenge of deciding when is the right time. I know that I have the leave this place that I am in presently, and I know that it is only a matter of time before it happens. God sends us clues and revelations when it is time to go and grow. He will make us so uncomfortable, that our only recourse will be to make the move. So what time is it for you? Is it time

Know What Time It Is

for you to write a book? Is it time for you to start a business? Is it time for you to back to school? You've been thinking about a change for a long time now! What are you waiting on? Now is the time for you to live out your dreams. When you step out on faith and make the move, God is waiting to catch you. The Lord delights in His people taking action and growing.

Even though a tree is planted in the ground, it still has branches that stretch out as wide as the tree continues to grow. This is what God wants you to do...stretch your branches (resources) and grow as tall as the tallest tree. We no longer live in a time where resources are as limited as they were in the past. Opportunities for us to start school, or even start a business are now easier than before. Extensive research may be required on your part, but the information is out there. Never be afraid to ask questions. Why? Because that's how you learn. There is really no such thing as a dumb question, because 9 times out of 10, there is someone else wanting to know the answer to the same question, but was afraid to ask. Weigh all of your options, and figure out what time it is!

Ecclesiastes 3
New International Version (NIV)

A Time for Everything

There is a time for everything,
and a season for every activity under the heavens:

a time to be born and a time to die,
a time to plant and a time to uproot,
a time to kill and a time to heal,
a time to tear down and a time to build,
a time to weep and a time to laugh,
a time to mourn and a time to dance,
a time to scatter stones and a time to gather them,
a time to embrace and a time to refrain from embracing,
a time to search and a time to give up,
a time to keep and a time to throw away,
a time to tear and a time to mend,
a time to be silent and a time to speak,
a time to love and a time to hate,
a time for war and a time for peace.

THE WOMAN I FELL IN LOVE WITH

IT IS TIME FOR ME TO...

CHAPTER

-5-

TRUST THE VISION

5

TRUST THE VISION

When God gives you a vision, He will also give you the provision associated with the vision. He will give and provide you with everything you need. God is a supplier of all your needs. Listen for the small voice and follow it. There will be times that you will doubt the direction of your life. However, once you develop a strong relationship with God, you will begin to trust His guidance. Before I moved to Atlanta, I must have heard that small, still voice over a thousand times saying, "go to Georgia." I would hear it and ignore it, or tell someone I was thinking of

THE WOMAN I FELL IN LOVE WITH

going to Georgia and they would talk me out of it. They'd ask questions like "what are you going to do there?" So because I was not sure of why God would be telling me to come back to Georgia, I would prolong and put it off. During this time, I had just graduated from Fayetteville State University with my Bachelors Degree and had been on a million interviews, still no job yet.

During this time, I was in a toxic relationship and really needed direction from God. So one day, I listened. I got the strength and the courage, I packed me and my 2 kids into my black 2008 BMW 328i and headed to Georgia. I went to visit my family, and they were surprised to see me home. So when they asked what I was doing home, I answered "oh just visiting".

I wasn't in Georgia 3 days and my phone started ringing with job opportunities. That's when I knew I was right where I was supposed to be. God had already aligned my path, All I had to do was to listen to the voice that was telling me the whole time to come to Georgia. Since I have been in Georgia, I have met some amazing people and could not be any happier. Now I am here and you are a part of my story. I know God has given you a vision for your life. There are some things that God have been tugging on you about and you have ignored the signs, or been outright disobedient. Remember that obedience is better than sacrifice. If God told you to do it, He will see you through.

Proverbs 29:18

Where there is no vision, the people perish.

THE WOMAN I FELL IN LOVE WITH

I KNOW GOD HAS BEEN TELLING ME TO:

CHAPTER

-6-

KEEP YOUR CUP FULL

6

KEEP YOUR CUP FULL

Keeping your cup full is another important principle to adopt in your day to day life. What do I mean when I say, "keep your cup full"? I mean your spiritual cup, which is your body. Change does not happen overnight, but it happens in small steps. That is why it is important to do something every day to keep your cup full. It is imperative that you start each day with a scripture and/or even a prayer. How you start your day usually determines how effective the rest of your day will be. I make it a habit to do

THE WOMAN I FELL IN LOVE WITH

something every day that will add value to the way I think and respond to situations that I will potentially face. Each day will not be easy; but if you are prepared to meet it with a positive affirmation, you will not easily succumb to the burdens and challenges associated with that day.

Other ways how you can keep your cup full is by looking at and listening to positive videos from your pastor or from other inspirational speakers such as myself. Some inspirational speakers that I personally listen to are T.D. Jakes, Steve Harvey, and Lisa Nichols...just to name a few. These are leaders who have played an intricate part of me ensuring my cup remains full at all times. Now, these are simple principles I apply to keep my cup full, but you just have to find what works for you. Make it your habit, and be intentional about it.

Keep Your Cup Full

List three things that you will commit to doing to keep your cup full.

I will keep my cup full by doing….

1. _____

2. _____

3. _____

Start doing them now, and be INTENTIONAL!

CHAPTER

-7-

BE A WOMAN OF INFLUENCE

7

BE A WOMAN OF INFLUENCE

A woman of influence is a woman who has established a relationship with God. Having a relationship with God is the first step in becoming a woman of influence. Without Him, you can never become a woman of influence. It is imperative that you establish this relationship with God as early in your life as possible. I remember establishing my relationship with God as early as 15 years old. At this age, I had already grown to recognize the presence of God in my life. I realized that God would be there when no one else would be. During these youthful and wonder years of my life, my parents were absent and living their own lives; and sometimes God was the only one who I could depend on. Another turning point in my life occurred at this tender age, as I became pregnant with my first son. There were times when I did not know what to do. I sought God for direction, and He was there to guide me through.

Having a Relationship with God

So what does it really mean to have a relationship with God? To have a relationship with God is similar to having a relationship with a companion, although it can seem peculiar in many ways. Even though you cannot see or touch God, you will know when He reveals Himself. God's presence has a strong spirit that will let you know when He enters the room. In order to have a strong relationship with God, there are many things you must do. The first thing...just like with any other relationship...is you must trust God. According to the Merriam Dictionary, to trust means to believe that something or someone is reliable, good, honest, and effective. God is all of those things, plus many more.

THE WOMAN I FELL IN LOVE WITH

SOME IMPORTANT STEPS I CAN TAKE TO BECOME A MORE INFLUENTIAL WOMAN:

_____

_____

_____

_____

_____

_____

CHAPTER

-8-

KNOW WHEN TO LET GO

8

KNOW WHEN TO LET GO

Letting go is one of the most powerful and liberating things that you can do in life. I remember a time in life that I was holding on to everything because I did not want to throw anything away. We tend to hold on to things with fear of losing them. What I have come to realize is that the more things we let go, the more that comes back to us. Even the things that hold no real value, we choose to hold on to them. We hold on to emotional baggage from the past, that is potentially damaging to our future. I'm not saying that those

THE WOMAN I FELL IN LOVE WITH

things were not painful or did not hurt us. We have the right to acknowledge the things that happen to us so that we never experience those things again. I called those things, "the hot stoves of life". In my teachings, I tell people that I have touched enough hot stoves during my life, and they really do burn!

When we let go of all the hurt and things that burned us, and turn them over to God, we then experience the true freedom that God always wanted us to have. It is one of the most freeing experiences to turn all of our problems, hurts, and past experiences over to God and let Him deal with them. Over the last couple of years of my life, I have learned to let go of anything that does not make me happy or feel good inside. This is to include any toxic relations, jobs, or people. I want to challenge you to let go of anything that no longer serves value to your life.

Know When To Let Go

List three things you will let go of:

1. _____

   _____

2. _____

   _____

3. _____

   _____

CHAPTER

-9-

BELIEVE IN YOURSELF

9

BELIEVE IN YOURSELF

Believing in yourself is another important attribute to have on your journey. You must be the first believer of yourself before anyone else will believe in you. We as women have what's called intuition, and it leads us through the path of life. Following your own intuition and believing in yourself will save you from a lot of heartache and pain. I can't tell you how many times I doubted myself, and talked myself out of something good because I didn't believe in myself. I first wanted to believe in the job, boyfriend, husband...and even sometimes friends before I first believed

THE WOMAN I FELL IN LOVE WITH

in myself. If I had acquired the attribute of believing in myself early on in life, it would not have taken this long to write a book or start a business.

I have always possessed strong faith in God and believed that He would see me through any situation. The thing about God is that He can't move unless you move. God is not going to magically show up in your life without action from you. Faith without works is dead. You should be your #1 supporter. If you think it, you can achieve it. The process may be long and it may not happen overnight, but if you keep the faith and believe in yourself, any vision that comes to mind will come to pass.

> ## Hebrews 11:6
>
> *But without faith; it is impossible to please Him*

CHAPTER

-10-

DON'T GIVE UP

10

DON'T GIVE UP

Don't give up on your dreams. There were so many times on my journey when I wanted to give up. But, every time I was tempted to do so, I always remembered my *"why"*. What is your *"why"*? Think about why you started your journey to accomplish your dreams in the first place. My children are my *"why"*. They are the reason I get up in the morning when I want to stay sleep. They are the reason why I joined the military, and they are the same reason I got out of the military. I joined so that they could experience a life different than the one I had. Four years later, I was getting out so that I could be a better mother and care for them. They are the reason I pushed through college to show them what's possible if you don't give up. They are definitely the reason why I chose to complete this book.

My proudest moment has been when my daughter asked me if she could read my book. I don't know how anyone else feels about that, but that filled my heart with gratitude. Her request meant more than anything to me. I know that this is just the beginning of many books that she will read, but I hope this one has the biggest impact.

Don't Give Up

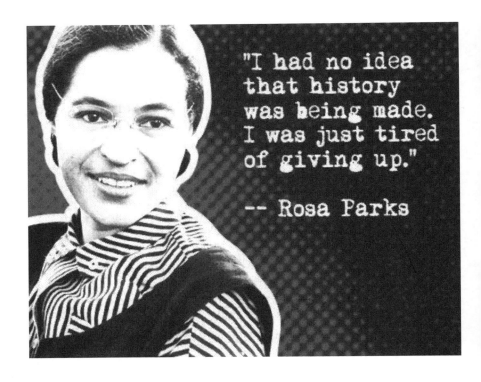

List 3 dreams you gave up on and need to reconsider pursuing again:

1. _____

2. _____

3. _____

CHAPTER

-11-

SHOW UP

11

SHOW UP

Another principle is to show up. Showing up is half the battle. You have to show up in your own life if you want to be successful at anything in life itself. You are the best representation of yourself and the way that you display yourself is the way the world sees you. How do you want to be seen in the word? Mark Twain was quoted as saying *"a man who lives fully is prepared to die."* So in life, you have a birthdate and a death date. What you do in between those dates are the things that matter. What will you do to make a difference in your own life? What will you do to make a difference in the lives of the people around you? It's time to get busy and put in the work for your life. If you don't like something, change it. If you can't change it, change your attitude about it. Let's say that you have some weight loss goals that you want to reach by the end of the year. You first have to know how many pounds you want to lose.

Use the S.M.A.R.T goal system to get started. The "S" stands for "specific"; so you have to have a specific number of pounds that you want to lose. The next letter, "M", stands for "measurable". You have to be able to measure your goals. Let's say you want to lose 30 pounds in 6 months. That can be a measure on a weekly or monthly basis, which will give you the ability to track your goals and see if you are on the right track. If you are not seeing results, maybe you need to make some adjustments. The "A" stands for "attainable". Is it possible to lose 30 pounds in 6 months? I think that it is very attainable if you set a goal to lose 5 pounds per month. The "R" stands for "realistic", and we have already discovered that is it realistic to lose 30 pounds in 6 months. The last letter, "T", stands for "time"...as in time-bound goal that can easily be reached in the amount of time that has been set. So after going through these goals, the most important thing is to show up and meet the upcoming challenges head-on. Come up with a strategic plan to reach these goals, like changing your diet or going for a daily run.

There will be days that you will not always get to do the plan, but do not detour away from it. The days that you miss or mess up, blow it off and keep going. Don't beat yourself up and allow yourself to feel like a failure. Even the greatest people in the world make mistakes. Dr. Martin Luther King, Jr. said that *if you can't fly, then run; if you can't run, then walk; if you can't walk, then crawl.*

The point of this is that you can do something to show up in your own life and make small steps to help you reach your goals. Showing up in your own life is one of the

THE WOMAN I FELL IN LOVE WITH

most remarkable things you can do for self-love and self-worth. Showing up helps you build the confidence you need. As you check your goals off your list, you start to realize that you can do so much more. So today, I challenge you to start showing up in your own life and watch how far you can go. It's all a balancing act, so balance it all out with a sustainable plan. Fall down, get back up. Make some mistakes. It's all a part of living!

CHAPTER

-12-

SET STANDARDS

12

SET STANDARDS

You should always set standards and have boundaries for your life. Set a standard for your life and stand on it! Don't allow anyone to come in your life and personal space with extra drama. Stop it at the door! Having standards keeps you from making bad decisions because you already know what you will and will not tolerate. Boundaries protect you from the things or people that come in your inner space to try to tear or break you down. Boundaries also help you stay centered. One of the boundaries I had to set up in my personal life was concerning

THE WOMAN I FELL IN LOVE WITH

my children. As soon as I would walk into the house from work, they would bomb-rush me at the door to update me about all of their activities and shenanigans. I was so overwhelmed with the information they were giving me, that I wasn't consciously retaining all of it.

As a result, I informed them that they had to give me at least 10 minutes to wind down once I came home from work. This allowed me the mental space to be receptive to the things they needed to share with me. We inevitably teach people how to treat us by our actions and by being proactive. Just something as simple as that allows me to be more loving and caring for my children.

Another boundary that one should consider setting is in the dating world. For instance, if you are considering dating someone who is already socially or romantically involved with another person, don't entertain them. If the only time the person you're dating calls you is late at night, set a boundary and let them know that if they can't call you—or only wants to be seen with you at night, you should

Set Standards

reconsider pursuing anything further with them. Have these boundaries in place to protect yourself from getting hurt. I'm not encouraging you to walk around with a long list of rules; but be wise enough to know what works for you and what doesn't.

CHAPTER

-13-

HAVE FAITH

13

HAVE FAITH

Have faith in the powers that be. You must have faith to accomplish the dreams and desires of your heart. The bible states that *"now faith is the substance of things hoped for, the evidence of things not seen."* I consider faith to be an imaginary picture of the way your life can be. Having faith in God is what allowed me to keep going when I could not see my way through tough situations such as financial issues, divorce, and many other obstacles. When times get tough (and they will!), you just have to keep the faith and believe that everything is working out for your good no matter what. Obstacles are a part of life that we just cannot avoid.

Everyone goes through something challenging at one point or another in their lifetime; but it is having faith that brings them through. As I am writing this book, there are many things going on in my personal life that I could let detour me from living my dreams. I have decided that no matter how it all turns out, everything will be alright. We have to go through the storms of life to get to the side of sunny days. Once you come out on the sunny side, things seem to get a little bit better.

I know that it's hard when you are in a difficult situation to believe that it will work out in your favor. That's where your faith kicks in and you hang on to that inch of belief. Sometimes what appears to be a problem or roadblock is something that is saving you from the trouble ahead. Have you ever been late for an appointment, but then as you ride down the road, you see an accident ahead? Sometimes God is protecting us from the accident ahead. You just have to trust the process, and in the meantime work on your faith. Work on your faith while you wait on God to unfold the promises of your life. You must have faith that the promises are there and are real in order for them to manifest.

> *Hebrews 11:1*
>
> *Now faith is the substance of things hoped for; the evidence of things not seen.*

CHAPTER

-14-

NEVER SETTLE

14

NEVER SETTLE

Never settle for less than God's best for you. The life that God has for you is much bigger than you can ever imagine. Sometimes we settle for less because we want what we are believing for right now! However, if we are patient and wait on God, He will surpass your thoughts. The bible speaks of us having a life of abundance, and that is what you should have. I'm not saying that we can't be content with what we already have; nevertheless, we should always be striving to be more than mediocre; and have the

THE WOMAN I FELL IN LOVE WITH

best life we can possibly have. It is easy to get comfortable in the place you are, and arrive to the conclusion that life has limited resources. Seek God for His resources. He knows what you need and is waiting to give you the life you deserve.

How do you know when you are settling? When you find yourself unhappy or blame others for why you have not accomplished your goals. You keep saying things like, *one day I will do this*, or *one day I will do that*. "One day" is not on the calendar. You have to make up in your mind that the time is now! Never be afraid of change. I have made many changes in my life. Some of the changes were good, and the others not so good; but with each decision, I learned something valuable.

In life, you have to be willing to take risks. The conditions may never be perfect for you to make the right move, but what if you never make it? You will never know what is possible. You don't want to live a life full of regrets, wishing that you should have done something differently.

Do not waste any more time wishing and wanting, when you can go out and create the life you deserve. Your biggest blessings are found outside your comfort zones. When God wants you to grow, He will make you uncomfortable. Is there a nagging feeling on the inside that you can't seem to understand or make sense of? That is God wanting you to grow, SO GO FOR IT. LET IT CHANGE YOUR LIFE!!!

> **There is no passion to be found in playing small—in settling for a life that is less than the one you are capable of living.**
>
> - Nelson Mandela

THE WOMAN I FELL IN LOVE WITH

5 things I promise myself that I will GO FOR starting TODAY:

1. _____

2. _____

3. _____

4. _____

5. _____

My Family...

Kedra and her children

Dre, Jada, & Javares

Dre, Javares, and Jada

Kedra and her daughter Jada

BIO

Kedra Banning is a woman of purpose, passion and motivation. She serves as a motivational speaker, life & business coach, and women's empowerment advocate. "Kedra Speaks" is how she communicates on social media outlets. Kedra became a mom at the age of 16 and instantly had to figure out parenting and deal with the challenges of adult life. She enjoys inspiring others through motivational and empowering messages. She received her B.S. in Business from Fayetteville State University in North Carolina. Kedra served 4 years in the military as a Human Resource Sergeant at Fort Bragg where she began motivating and speaking to others. In the military, she was chosen as the narrator and speaker for Chain of Command Ceremonies and other military events. Known for taking on challenges and maintaining focus, she made the rank of SGT in 2 years. Kedra has successfully faced many obstacles and hurdles, and she gives all credit to her faith and to God. Serving in the military taught her the leadership skills needed to become a successful business woman. She operated a successful gift basket business at Fort Bragg for over 5 years. She is an entrepreneur, speaker, business woman and author dedicated to helping others succeed. One of her upcoming projects is to open a non-profit organization to help women get the necessary skills to be successful in business & life.

She can be reached at:

Website: www.kedraspeaks1.com

Website: www.peopleprojectsprograms.com

Email: kedraspeaks@gmail.com

: www.facebook.com/kedraspeaks

NOTES:

- Love yourself before you attempt to love anyone else
- God allows you to take the long route so you can get to where he wants you to be
- Never let a situation or setback dictate your life
- Everything you are going through is preparing you for where you are meant to be
- Who you are inside is more important than what the outer appearance looks like
- Ask God to clean your heart!?!!!!!!!!
- Its not where you start, its how you finish
- Don't ever let your past determine your future
- Don't be afraid to ask questions?!?
- How you start your day effects how the rest of your day will turn out
- Each day wont be easy!!!
- Emotional Baggage
- Let go of anything that does not make me happy
- Believe in myself
- Think it you will achieve it

NOTES:

27:30 Leviticus Proverbs 39-10
Romans 11:16
3 John 1:2 Deuteronomy 12:11-12 Genesis 4:7-?
Malachi

Controlled by our will instead of being led by our Spirit

Mind
Will
Thoughts → My Self!!!!!
know-ledge(?)

• Giving vs Bringing

Upgrade your thinking
Previous way of thinking it has produced
the amount of provision in which you live

Tithing/offering = Get plan to prosper men
When you give God's way he'll give your way only

— we're not giving we're (returning) to God
what belongs to him

The only way you can qualify for a harvest is to plant a seed

10% of income

(Giving in faith)

NOTES:

Standards and boundaries
Dont live life full of regrets

NOTES:

Made in the USA
San Bernardino, CA
30 December 2016